PIANO PAINTINGS

16 INTERMEDIATE PIANO SOLOS FOR ART LOVERS

BARBARA ARENS & ALISON MATHEWS

Editions Rensakov

All pieces in this book can be heard on YouTube.

There is a web page dedicated to this book:

https://pianocreatives.weebly.com/piano-paintings.html

Here you will be able to listen to recordings made by the composers,
alongside the works of art that inspired the music.
You will also be able to explore all of our collaborative projects.
We'd love it if you would leave comments or share ideas there!

Scan the QR code to see all the artworks:

PIANO PAINTINGS

Editions Rensakov

©2019

CONTENTS

PIANO PAINTINGS - INTRODUCTORY NOTES

A Radiant Day - Alison Mathews

I discovered this American artist by accident and fell in love with his appealing naivety and joyful paintings of nature. In this oil painting Burchfield captures a wonderful feeling of space, light and warmth. Although the sun is out of sight, I can feel the warmth and radiance of the sun at high noon. I hope this, along with an uplifting feeling, can be felt in the music.

Charles E. Burchfield – Hill Top at High Noon 1925

Sketches of Clouds - Barbara Arens

John Constable's cloud sketches are so blowy, breezy and spontaneous – they're like a breath of fresh air. In some of the sketches he made of clouds over Hampstead Heath, we see how light wispy fragments build up into a towering cumulus. This is the idea I try to convey here.

John Constable – Clouds over Hampstead Heath 1822

The Woman in Gold - Alison Mathews

This opulent painting is a treat for the eye! It shimmers and shines with the gold and silver leaf used on the canvas, there are intricate designs on the elegant dress and the face of Adele Bloch-Bauer is beguiling. As well as trying to create a shimmering effect, I wanted to capture something of the poised and elegant woman who is enveloped in gold.

Gustav Klimt – Portrait of Adele Bloch-Bauer (also called The Woman in Gold) **1903-1907**

Grimshaw - Barbara Arens

The Victorian painter Atkinson Grimshaw's 'At the Park Gate' seems to tell a story: we see a moonlit night in winter – bare trees reach into the sky. Someone stands at the gate leading to a fine country house. For this person, that house is a haunted house, I feel; it is full of haunting memories.

Atkinson Grimshaw – At the Park Gate 1878

Constellation - Alison Mathews

One of a series of 23 small paintings, I saw these at an exhibition and fell in love with them. The intricate details, soft background, intersecting black lines are just like a weird astral map! I tried to recreate an overall soft, background harmony against which the melody interweaves like the black lines. The primary colours that pop out are described by solid chord progressions, which contrast with the more fluid parts of the piece.

Jean Miró – The Morning Star 1940

Far Away - Barbara Arens

'The Catskills' by Asher Brown Durand, of the Hudson River School, shows us a gorgeous pristine landscape, untouched by man. And more than that – our eye is led further and further, over the waterfall, along the valley, into the immense, yet undiscovered beauties far away!

Asher Brown Durand – The Catskills 1858

Heavy Machinery - Alison Mathews

The artist Léger was fascinated by machinery and technology. Here, the parts are frozen into an abstract design and yet I can imagine them working together to create a fantastic machine. In the music, I wanted to create a feeling of different elements being juxtaposed and plenty of movement.

Fernand Léger – Machine element 1st state 1924

Dance - Barbara Arens

Matisse's 'La Danse' is audaciously primitive. He only uses four bold colours: blue, green, orange-red and brown – Pop Art from 1909! Hence my choice of the 'primitive' four basic harmonies used in pop music. The dancers are going around and around – the music goes around and around…

Henri Matisse – La Danse 1909

Totes Meer - Alison Mathews

This painting, by the celebrated British war artist Nash, intrigues me – the imagery is powerful. The wrecks of German aircraft, photographed by Nash in a salvage dump, are transformed into a violent sea hemmed in by a desolate landscape. The colour of the sky, lit by a pale moon reflects that of the sea, ('Totes Meer' = Dead Sea) creating a mournful atmosphere. I hope the uneven rhythm, and at times, dissonant harmony in the music captures this!

Paul Nash – Totes Meer 1940-41

Birds in a Landscape with Waterfall - Barbara Arens

Visiting Japan as a child left me with vivid impressions of the country. The stylisation of Japanese art – be it in the medium of woodblock, ceramics, netsuke, or, as here, painted on a paper screen, has continued to fascinate me. In my piece, we hear the birds singing, the river flowing, and the extremely stylised waterfall rushing down.

Attrib. Kano Utanosuke – Japanese Birds and Flowers in a landscape - late 16th century

Waves in the Moonlight
- Barbara Arens

Who doesn't love Caspar David Friedrich! His romantic landscapes – with or without human figures – engage our imaginations in a unique way. Here he shows three figures – two sisters and their father? Watching the moon rise over the Baltic Sea, hearing the waves break on the stones where they are perched, and observing two ships – do they bear loved ones aboard?

Caspar David Friedrich
– Moonrise over the Sea 1822

Unspoken Thoughts
- Alison Mathews

One genre I greatly enjoy is illustrative art. Harry Clarke was one of the most prolific illustrators of the Irish Arts and Crafts movement. This comes from the book "The Little Mermaid" by Hans Christian Andersen. There is so much detail in this stylized drawing. I wanted to create a floating, ethereal feel set against a constant flowing of the water.

Harry Clarke – illustration "'I know what you want', said the sea witch" from 'The Little Mermaid' 1916

Speed - Alison Mathews

This painting is absolutely full of movement - a rush and swirl of colours, above which the cityscape rises. I hope that is also the music in a nutshell!

Leandro Manzo – Heavy Traffic 5 2009

Twilight over the Water
- Barbara Arens

I love the marvellous atmosphere in 'Twilight over the Water' by the American landscape painter Charles H. Davis. He basically uses only three colours: glowing gold, icy blue, and black; and with them creates an impressionist, very romantic mood.

Charles Harold Davis – Twilight over the Water 1892

Evening at the Window - Alison Mathews

This painting exudes romance along with a feeling of contentment and I can almost feel the warmth of a summer's evening through the open window. I like to imagine what the story is behind the couple reflected in the glass of the window. Are they real or is it a dream? Chagall once wrote "I had only to open my bed-room window and blue air, love and flowers entered with her".

Marc Chagall – Evening at the Window 1950

Koi - Barbara Arens

Escher's print 'Three Worlds' is, like so many of his works, totally mind-boggling. We're looking at a body of water – leaves float on the surface. But at the same time we see through the surface, into the depths, where a koi fish is swimming. AND at the same time we see the reflection of the bare trees whence the leaves came. Playing with these ideas from Escher's lithograph in real life, I was intrigued by the koi pond in the botanical gardens in Glasgow; my eye could wander from the water lilies on the surface, to the reflections cast by the palms and architecture, into the murky depths of the pond, where beautiful gold, silver and black koi appeared and disappeared again. My piece 'Koi' attempts to show these different levels; leaves or flowers floating on the surface, the fish gracefully weaving through the water, the murky deep, into which they disappear…

M.C. Escher – Three Worlds 1955

A Radiant Day

A. Mathews

Inspired by 'Hill Top at High Noon' by Charles E. Burchfield

Sketches of Clouds

Inspired by 'Clouds over Hampstead Heath' by John Constable

B. Arens

© 2018

The Woman in Gold

Inspired by the painting by Gustav Klimt

A. Mathews

Grimshaw

Inspired by 'At the Park Gate' by Atkinson Grimshaw

B. Arens

©2018

Constellation

Inspired by 'The Morning Star' by Joan Miró

A. Mathews

With an air of mystery and wonder ♩ c. 120

Far Away

Inspired by 'The Catskills' by Asher Brown Durand

B. Arens

Heavy Machinery

Inspired by 'Machine element 1st state' by Fernand Léger

A. Mathews

Dance

Inspired by 'La Danse' by Henri Matisse

B. Arens

Totes Meer

Inspired by the painting by Paul Nash

A. Mathews

Birds in a Landscape with Waterfall

Inspired by 'Japanese Birds and Flowers in a Landscape'
attributed to Kano Utanosuke

B. Arens

© 2018

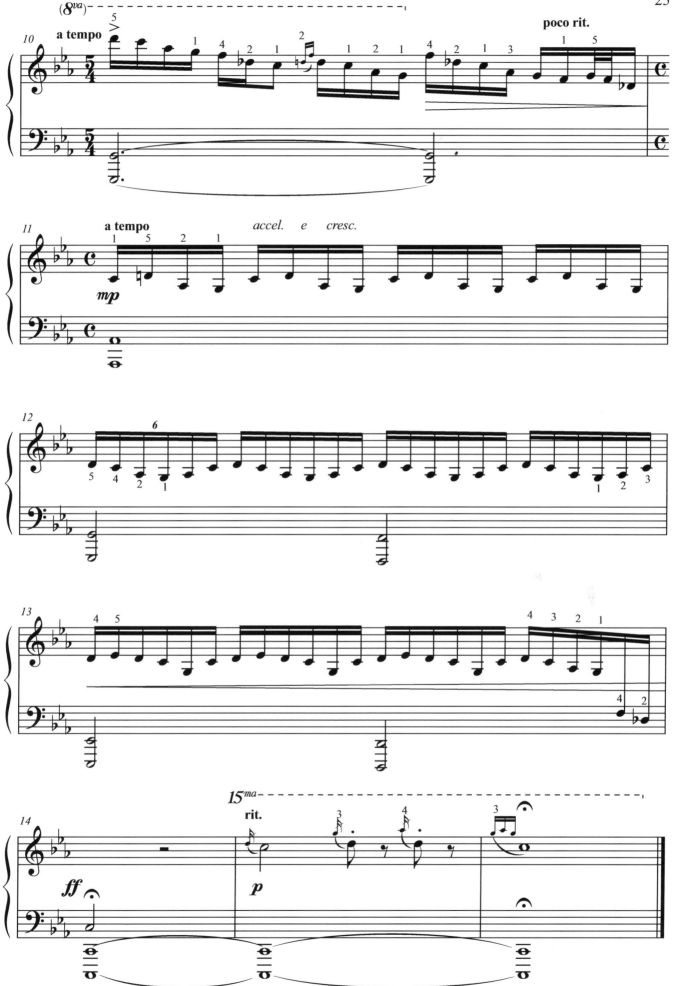

Unspoken Thoughts

Inspired by Harry Clarke's illustrations to 'The Little Mermaid'   A. Mathews

Speed

Inspired by 'Heavy Traffic' by Leandro Manzo

A. Mathews

With Drive ♩ = 184

con Ped.

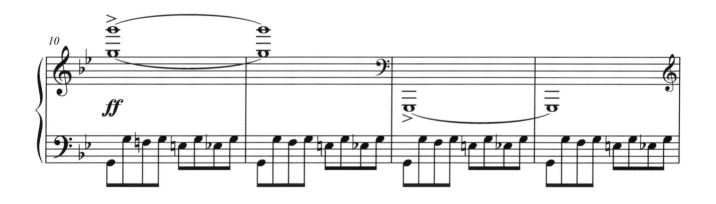

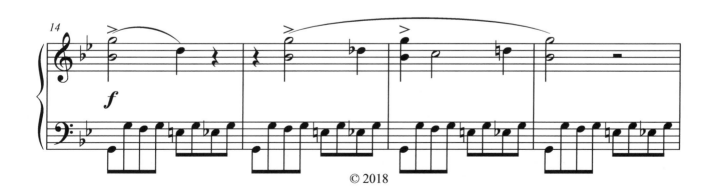

© 2018

Waves in the Moonlight

Inspired by 'Mondaufgang am Meer' by Caspar David Friedrich

B. Arens

© 2018

Twilight over the Water

Inspired by the painting by Charles H. Davis

B. Arens

Evening at the Window

Inspired by the painting by Marc Chagall

A. Mathews

Contented, with rubato ♩ = 80

Koi

Inspired by M.C. Escher's lithograph '3 Worlds'

B. Arens

ALISON MATHEWS is a classically trained pianist and graduate of the Royal College of Music with both a MMus and teaching diploma. With the philosophy of music at the heart of her studies she completed a masters degree at Surrey University and was then offered a scholarship to pursue a Doctorate. Having a family intervened and she went on to build a highly regarded private teaching practice whilst developing a series of composition workshops for young pianists. Her interest in composition grew from a desire to provide students with imaginative educational music that explored the full range and sonority of the piano.

With Editions Musica Ferrum she has published:

Treasure Trove

Capturing the Spirit of Christmas

Capturing the Joy of Winter

Doodles

Mosaic Vol 1

Mosaic Vol 2

Other publications include **Piano Planets** with EVC Publications and being included in the collection **Small Hand Piano** with Breitkopf & Härtel. Her music is also due to be included in the Irish Royal Academy of Music piano syllabus for 2020.

BARBARA ARENS is an enthusiastic piano teacher. She began her studies at the Mozarteum in Salzburg at the age of 13. After a concert career performing primarily as harpsichordist and organist, she now enjoys composing for her piano pupils. She presently lives near Würzburg, Germany, after living in Beirut, Dallas, San Francisco, Singapore, Salzburg, London and Munich.

She has published the following books with Breitkopf & Härtel:

One Hand Piano

21 Amazingly Easy Pieces

Piano Misterioso

Piano Vivace/Piano Tranquillo

Piano Exotico

Small Hand Piano

With Editions Musica Ferrum London, she has published

Rendezvous with Midnight: 12+1 Nocturnes for Teens

All Beautiful & Splendid Things: 12+1 Songs for Piano on Poems by Women

Capturing the Spirit of Christmas and

Capturing the Joy of Winter in collaboration with Alison Mathews.

With Spartan Press Music she published her

Scottish Collection and

The More the Merrier: 13 Duets for 4-Hand Piano & Everyone Else

With Editions Rensakov at Amazon, she has published as paperbacks and as Kindle e-books:

Fast & Furioso – 13 Fast & Furious Pieces for Piano

Dreaming at the Piano - 12 musing, meditative piano pieces for the intermediate pianist

The Herakles Challenge – 12 Epic tasks for Piano based on Greek Mythology

Chubby Hippo & Friends – 10 Really Easy Piano Pieces with Really Silly Lyrics

Grand Piano – A Pot-Pourri of seven early-advanced Pieces

The Vampire Challenge – Count Dracula's Piano Book

The Mermaid Challenge – 12 Piano Pieces requiring collaborative effort!

All the World's Stage – 13 Shakespeare Characters for solo piano

Printed in Great Britain
by Amazon